DISCARDED

574.5
P   Pringle, Laurence

     The hidden World;
     life under a rock

DATE DUE

LOWER DAUPHIN SCHOOL DISTRICT
East Hanover Library

The Hidden World

LIFE UNDER A ROCK

By Laurence Pringle

MACMILLAN PUBLISHING CO., INC.
NEW YORK
COLLIER MACMILLAN PUBLISHERS
LONDON

Copyright © 1977 Laurence Pringle
Copyright © 1977 Macmillan Publishing Co., Inc.
All rights reserved. No part of this book may be reproduced or transmitted in any form or by any means, electronic or mechanical, including photocopying, recording or by any information storage and retrieval system, without permission in writing from the Publisher.

Macmillan Publishing Co., Inc.
866 Third Avenue, New York, N.Y. 10022
Collier Macmillan Canada, Ltd.

Drawings on pages 8, 15, 28, 33, 35, 39, 47, 48, 52, 58 by Erick Ingraham
Designed by Bobye List
PRINTED IN THE UNITED STATES OF AMERICA

10 9 8 7 6 5 4 3 2 1

Library of Congress Cataloging in Publication Data
Pringle, Laurence P
   The hidden world.
   Bibliography: p.
   Includes index.
   SUMMARY: A guide to the most common plants and animals one may find under rocks, logs, and other objects on land and in water.
   1. Cryptozoa—Juvenile literature.   [1. Animals.
2. Cryptozoa.   3. Plants]   I. Ingraham, Erick.   II. Title.
QL110.P74   574.5'26   76-47641   ISBN 0-02-775340-9

About This Book

An ecosystem is a place in nature with all of its living and nonliving parts. Ecosystems are all around us. Some are big, some are little. The planet earth is one ecosystem; a rotting log is another. Ponds, forests, and backyards are ecosystems too.

This book is about very small ecosystems—the ones that exist under rocks, logs, boards, and other objects that rest on the soil, both on land and in water. At first glance, these objects seem hardly worth noticing—they are just part of the landscape; something to step over, or around, or on. If you tip over a few rocks, however, you will see a world that is very different from the surroundings just a few inches away. The special environment under rocks is ideal for many kinds of animals. Some scientists call it the *cryptosphere*, which means "hidden world."

This book is a guide to some of the most common kinds of animals and plants you may find under rocks and other objects. There is a lot to learn about this ecosystem and its life. The hidden world is a fascinating place to explore.

IT IS AN AUGUST AFTERNOON, HOT AND DRY. No rain has fallen for many days. The ground is dusty; most people's lawns are turning brown. To cool off, some people use air conditioners or go swimming. Others just wait for the cool of evening.

Other animals avoid the heat and dryness by living under rocks and other objects on the ground. Little animals gather there, sometimes by the hundreds. There are sowbugs, slugs, centipedes, beetles, ants, crickets, and earwigs. These and dozens of other kinds of animals thrive in the special environment under rocks. These animals might not exist at all without this hidden world ecosystem.

The climate under a rock is cool and damp. Some animals need this microclimate ("little climate") in order to survive, and to raise their young. They can't live for long in the hot, dry climate of the soil surface that is just a short distance away.

A stone blocks the direct rays of the sun from the soil beneath it. No breezes reach the soil, either, so very little water escapes into the air. Sometimes the underside of a rock actually glistens with water droplets. Plants often grow in a kind of necklace around the rock—perhaps because they, too, thrive in the moisture of the hidden world. Their stems

and leaves shield part of the rock from the sun, and so they also help maintain the special microclimate. In fact, the climate underneath these plants, near the border of the soil and the rock, is often very much like that beneath the rock. You may find little animals hiding in this border area.

The hidden world is dark, and some animals stay in dim light all of the time. They may creep out from underneath stones at night. The hidden world is also a safe place, a shelter where little animals are protected somewhat from larger animals that might eat them. However, some hunters, such as shrews, are attracted to this world by the abundance of life there.

Hidden world ecosystems are found not only under rocks but also under boards, piles of firewood, pieces of cloth and metal, and even under old newspapers or flattened cardboard cartons. Any object that covers an area of the ground will do.

You can easily create this special environment. Put a cinder block, a good-sized stone, piece of wood, or other object on the ground in a lawn, field, garden, or woods. Leave it for a week. Then turn it over and compare that spot with the earth around it. What has happened to plants that were covered? Feel the soil and compare it with earth where the sun has shone.

Very likely, some animals have already gathered under the object. Some may be on the ground, or in burrows they dug there. Others may cling to the underside of the shelter itself. Put the shelter back in the same spot. Then you can check it in the weeks ahead, and see whether the numbers and kinds of animals change.

In the hidden world you will also see animals that normally live underground. You will probably find earthworms under rocks. In order to keep their skins moist in dry seasons, earthworms ordinarily burrow deep into the soil. But rocks and other objects provide oases near the surface. You may also see springtails under stones, though you will have to look closely. They are only an eighth of an inch long. Other animals are even smaller, so a magnifying glass will help as you explore the hidden world.

Although biologists have studied the lives of individual animals that are commonly found under rocks, there have been very few studies of an entire hidden world ecosystem. One biologist studied the climate under rocks in Arizona. He measured both the temperature and the humidity (the amount of water vapor in the air). In one area he found that the general humidity of the air was 64 percent, while

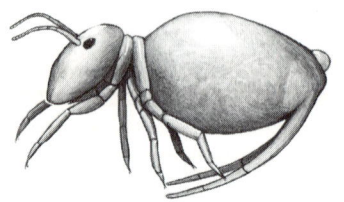

A snap of the springlike device under a springtail flips the animal through the air.

the humidity under a rock was much higher—78 percent. In another part of Arizona the air humidity was 77 percent. Under a small rock the air was just a little more humid, but under a large rock the humidity was 83 percent.

Ordinarily, the temperature and humidity of the air change from day to day, and also vary between night and day. The biologist found that the temperature and humidity under rocks did not change nearly as much as in the open air. The conditions under rocks were usually the best available for many kinds of little animals. So, even in the Arizona desert, hidden world ecosystems provide cool, damp microclimates.

Even on other planets, the environment under rocks is considered a special place by scientists. In 1976, the Viking 2 lander extended its metal arm, scooped up a sample of soil from Mars, and brought it into the spacecraft for chemical testing. No signs of living organisms were found. But the investigation did not stop there. If any signs of life were to be found, the scientists reasoned, the best place to look was under Martian rocks. They might serve as a shield from the very strong ultraviolet sun rays that strike the surface of Mars. So the mechanical arm of Viking 2 tipped over some rocks and took soil samples from underneath. Unfortunately, there were still no signs of present or past life.

Life in the hidden world varies from place to place, and even between objects that are only a few inches apart. To investigate an area, first make a simple map that shows the position of each good-sized rock, board, or other object on the ground. Take notes about the kinds and numbers of animals you find under each object. Always replace the rock in the same position so that the area is disturbed as little as possible. Look under the rocks during different seasons and in different kinds of weather. With a flashlight you can observe the hidden world life at night too, and compare it with what you find during the day.

Listing the animals you find can be fun, but this is just a first step in studying an ecosystem. Try to find out how animals depend on one another, and on other parts of their environment. For example, you will find that some rocks or other objects are settled tightly into the soil, while others rest more lightly on the ground. How does this affect the kinds of animals you find? What effects do the shape and size of stones have on their animal life? Do rocks with bumpy surfaces attract different kinds or numbers of animals than rocks with smooth surfaces?

You may see one kind of animal eating another. Which kinds of animals seem to live together "peacefully"? You might also want to investigate the travels of hidden world animals. Mark the backs of some sowbugs or beetles with quick-drying nail polish of a bright color. Note the location of their rocks on your map. Then watch for these individuals on the following days.

Harmless garter snakes (right) and lizards often rest under rocks.

Almost every stone you turn over will offer a surprise. Usually it will be a pleasant surprise, because nearly all animals that live under rocks are harmless to humans. But some may be dangerous, so use caution and common sense as you explore. Stay away from places where you see bees flying to and from a hole beneath a rock or near one. Bees such as yellow jackets sometimes live in such places and they may

sting you if their nest is disturbed. Be especially careful if you live in a region where poisonous snakes or scorpions exist. However, the presence of these animals need not keep you from exploring under rocks and other objects. Snakes and scorpions avoid people as best they can. You can help them avoid you by using a stick, rather than your fingers, to tip over a rock that seems big enough to offer them shelter.

Throughout North America, most hidden world animals you find will be harmless and safe to pick up, though it is wise to use forceps (tweezers) for this at first. Some people shudder at the thought of touching small, "crawly" animals. As you learn more about these animals and discover which kinds are harmless, you may want to touch some of them. However, try to disturb them and their hidden world as little as possible.

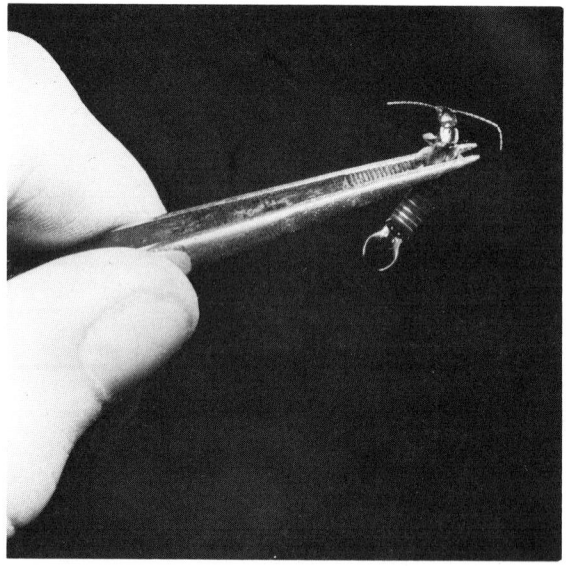

Forceps holding an earwig, which can pinch fingers

Some of the most common kinds of animals and plants are shown on the following pages. They exist almost everywhere—in backyards, city lots, gardens, school grounds, parks, as well as in the country. There is a hidden world right at your feet, waiting to be explored.

Sowbugs

Sowbugs are among the most abundant and common animals in the hidden world. In England they are called wood lice, though they are not lice. Neither are they bugs. These small slate-gray animals are relatives of crabs, shrimps, and lobsters. Biologists call them isopods because they are in the group Isopoda, part of a class of animals called crustaceans.

Some kinds of sowbugs can roll up tightly in a ball to protect themselves. They're called pill bugs.

A pill bug partly curled into its "pill" shape

There are also seacoast isopods that hide under rocks and other shelter near oceans, but many other kinds live inland. They have escaped from a watery life, but not from a great need for water. The air they breathe must be humid. So they keep out of direct sunlight, stay in damp microclimates, and venture out at night or on cloudy or rainy days.

A California biologist marked some sowbugs and noticed how their travels varied with the weather. They moved very little in the rainy season; one traveled just 10 meters (about 32 feet) in 6 days. During dry weather, however, two sowbugs moved 13 meters (about 51 feet) in just one night. The biologist concluded that the sowbugs were having difficulty finding the microclimate they needed. So, whenever he needed some animals for his studies, he wet a patch of soil, placed a board over it, and the next day had plenty of sowbugs.

Sowbugs are usually scavengers—eaters of dead plants and animals. They feed on bits of grass, fallen tree leaves, fungi, and small dead creatures. Sometimes they graze on algae that grow on rocks. And sometimes they are predators, attacking small animals (including young sowbugs) and eating them.

Under a rock you may see what looks like dead sowbugs lying about. These may be cast-off sowbug "skins" that were outgrown and molted. Sowbugs sometimes eat their old "skins." And sowbugs themselves are food for such predators as beetles, spiders, toads, shrews, and lizards.

Millipedes and Centipedes

Millipedes and centipedes look somewhat like worms—long and slender—but they are named for their many legs. Millipede means "thousand legs" and centipede means "hundred legs." In both cases they have many fewer. Most kinds of centipedes have about 35 body segments with a pair of legs on each one. Millipedes have two pairs of legs per segment, and most species have a hundred or fewer segments.

The bodies of most millipedes are rounded and look like the hoses that attach to vacuum cleaners. In order to protect themselves they sometimes roll quickly into a tight coil. Their feet and mouths are tucked safely inside. A predator is faced with a smooth, hard outer surface that is difficult to grip. Millipedes also repel predators with a bitter-smelling brown liquid, which is released from tiny sacs within their body segments. They are scavengers, eating partly decayed leaves and the fungi that grow on the leaves.

The bodies of centipedes are flattened, and their legs stick out to the side. They are able to squeeze into narrow spaces under rocks. Some burrow like earthworms in the soil. Centipedes can move quickly, and are among the main predators of the hidden world. They have poison fangs, and large centipedes can give a painful bite. The bite of a centipede kills such prey as insects and earthworms. Since they spend most of their lives in darkness and dim light, centipedes find their prey by smell and perhaps by touch.

Slugs and Snails

Slugs are mollusks, related to snails, oysters, and clams. Unlike nearly all mollusks, they have little or no shell; otherwise they are quite similar to snails. To keep their skins moist they must live in cool, damp places. In the evenings or on cloudy days they creep out from under rocks, traveling on a trail of slime that their body produces. They are scavengers, but also eat parts of live plants.

The shells of land snails protect them from drying out. Slugs lack this protection, so on sunny days you will find them under rocks or clinging right near the border between a rock and the soil. Watch for clusters of round, cream-colored slug eggs under stones too. They look like little

Clusters of slug eggs are stuck together with slime.

pearls. Often as many as fifty are laid in a cluster. A parent slug gives the eggs no care, so their survival depends mostly on the microclimate in which they are left. If it stays cool and moist for about a month, little slugs emerge from the eggs.

Spiders

More than a hundred species of spiders may live on an acre of land. In some ways, each species is different from the others. They may be active at different times of the day. They eat different kinds of food. They catch it in different ways. And they live in different places. At least part of the time, some live in the hidden world.

Though you will find small webs under rocks, most of the spiders there are not web-spinners. They are hunters, not trappers. They still produce silk, however, and use it to wrap their prey or to spin protective burrows or egg cases. You will often find egg cases attached to the underside of rocks and other objects.

Wolf spiders usually live on the ground. They often rest or hunt under rocks.

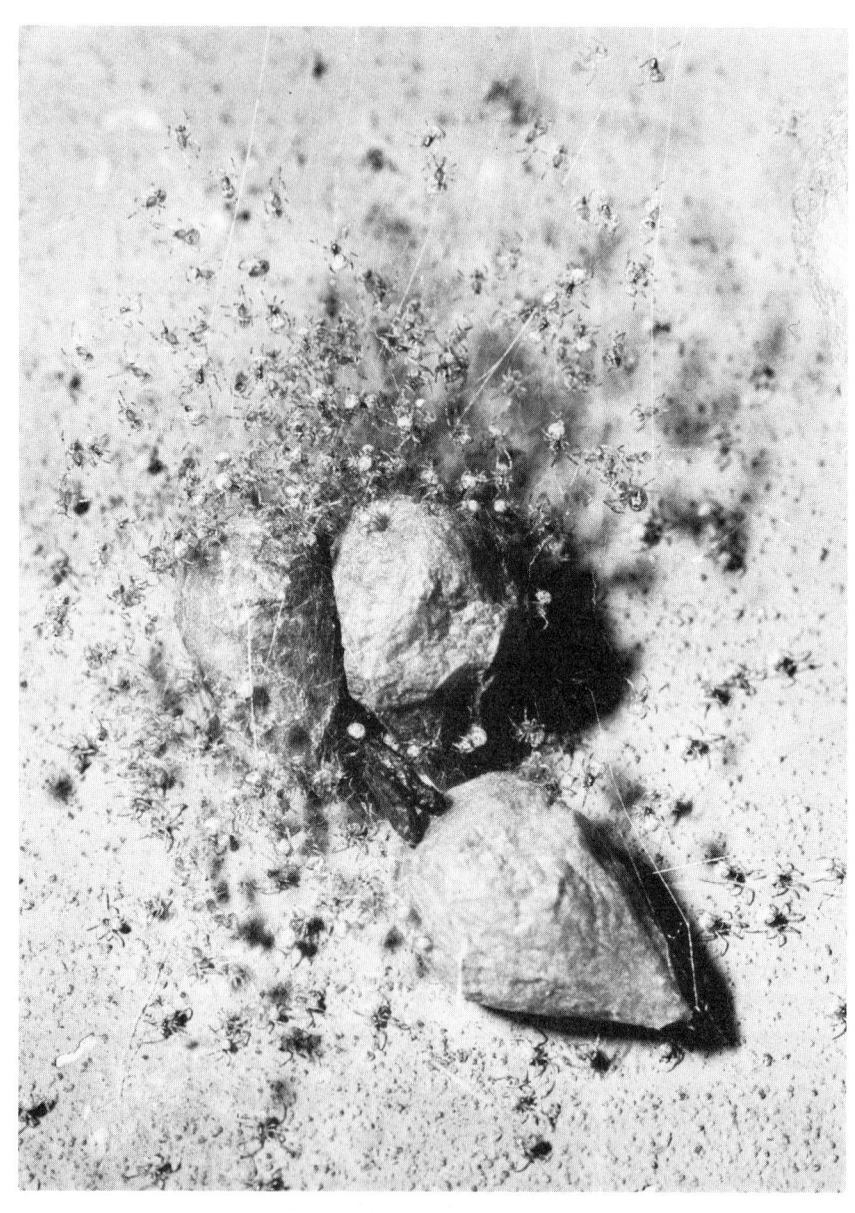
Spiderlings emerging from egg cases

Many kinds of dwarf spiders live under rocks. Most of them are no more than a tenth of an inch (two millimeters) long. A large spider (a half inch long) called Dysdera has long jaws that are especially suited for catching sowbugs, a favorite food. The hidden world is also home for wolf spiders. These spiders are fast-moving predators with keen vision. Some of them dig burrows in the soil under rocks. You can lure them out by gently poking a twig or straw into their hideout.

Some kinds of spiders spin webs close to stones. Part of the web is a funnel-shaped structure that leads to, or under, the rock. This is the spider's refuge; it dashes out when an insect or other prey touches the web.

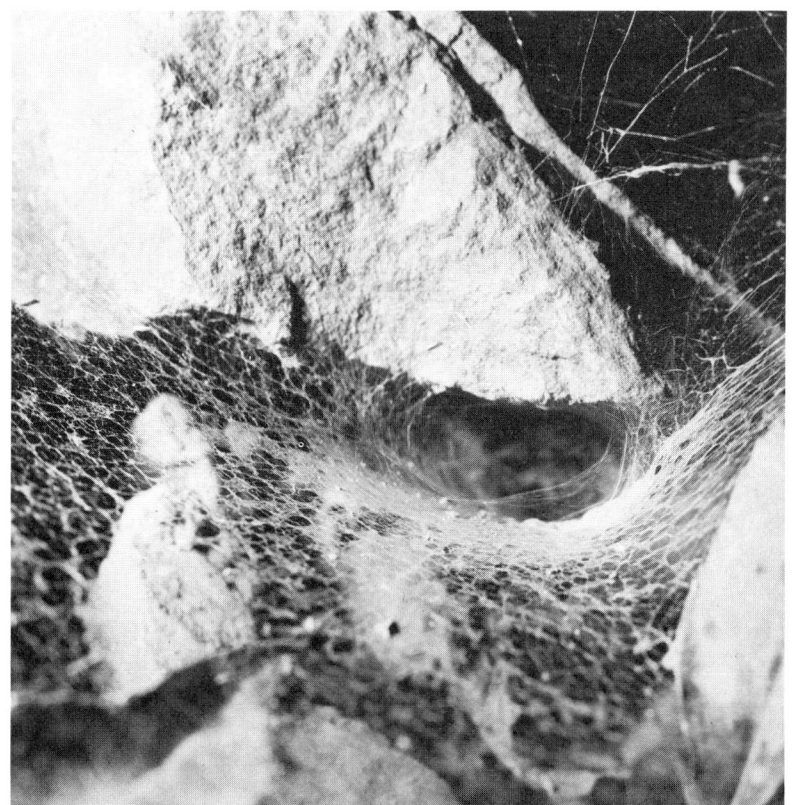

In all, there are several hundred different kinds of spiders that spend part of their lives in the hidden world. Almost all of them are harmless to people. The fangs of many species are too small to cut into human skin. However, the black widow and brown recluse spiders have poison that affects people, and they sometimes live under objects, especially near buildings. It is wise not to touch or pick up any spider with your fingers.

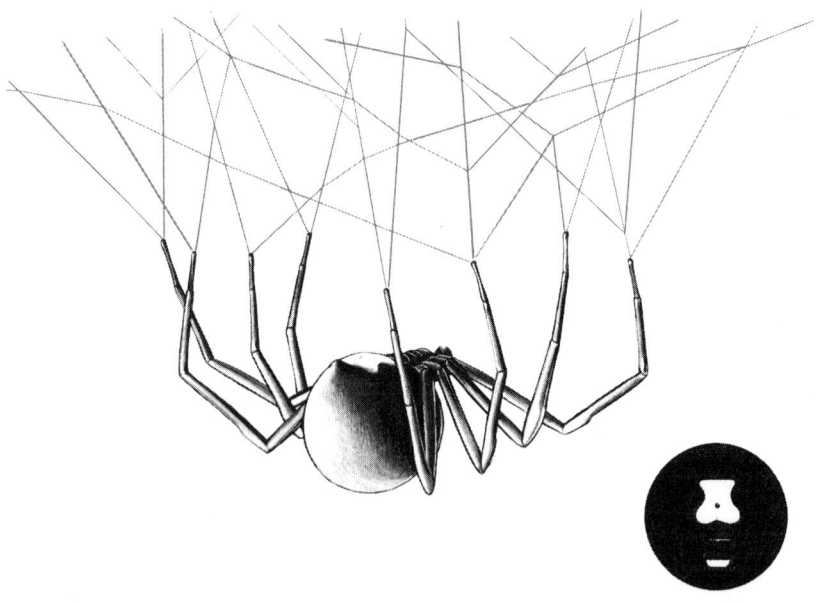

The poisonous black widow spider lives under objects. It has a distinctive red hourglass shape on its underside.

Ants

As you turn over rocks in the summertime, you are almost certain to find ants. When sunlight strikes the hidden world, worker ants rush around. They pick up light-colored "eggs" in their jaws and carry them to safety under another rock or down tunnels that lead underground. Actually the eggs of most ants are quite tiny, and the clusters of whitish objects you see are probably pupae in their cocoons. If you cut open a cocoon and look with a magnifying glass, you will see a pupa inside. It is the last stage of development before an ant becomes an adult.

Ants with clusters of tiny eggs.

Ants tending young aphid "slaves" under a rock

In an ant colony, the workers take care of the eggs, larvae, and pupae. They move them around, not just in emergencies, but in day-to-day life. In order to develop properly, the eggs and other early stages of ant life must be kept in a certain microclimate. So workers may carry them deep underground, or up near the surface, depending on changes in the temperature and humidity.

Ants are the favorite food of the flicker—a woodpecker that commonly feeds on the ground. If you see a flicker exploring the edges of rocks, you can be sure that there are—or were—ants there. The flicker catches them with its long, sticky tongue.

Crickets

A boy wanted some live food for his pet lizard, and he knew exactly where to get it. He walked along the edge of a road, near some railroad tracks, and lifted up loose rocks, pieces of wood, and old cardboard cartons that lay there. Underneath these objects he found plenty of crickets, a favorite food of his lizard.

Male field crickets make their distinctive chirping sounds by rubbing their front wings together.

Camel crickets have long hind legs and antennae.

Most people recognize the black or dark brown field cricket. Its body is rather plump, so this insect hides under rocks and other objects that have a "loose fit" with the earth. When you look under rocks you may also find other, less-well-known crickets. Mole crickets burrow underground and eat plant roots. The camel cricket is also a skillful digger. All crickets are scavengers.

Earwigs

The earwig is also a scavenger, and a plant-eater. It is probably the scariest-looking insect found under rocks. Sharp pincers stick out behind its abdomen, and these pincers can pinch! (You can tell the sexes apart by their pincers: those of males are much more curved than those of females.) Earwigs also defend themselves with a foul-smelling liquid.

Earwigs spend the day in dark, damp microclimates. In the soil under rocks, female earwigs dig little holes and lay their eggs. They guard the eggs, and rearrange them from time to time. This probably helps prevent the growth of mold on the eggs. Some kinds of female earwigs also care for their young after they hatch. Watch for a mother earwig and her tiny young (called nymphs) when you look under rocks.

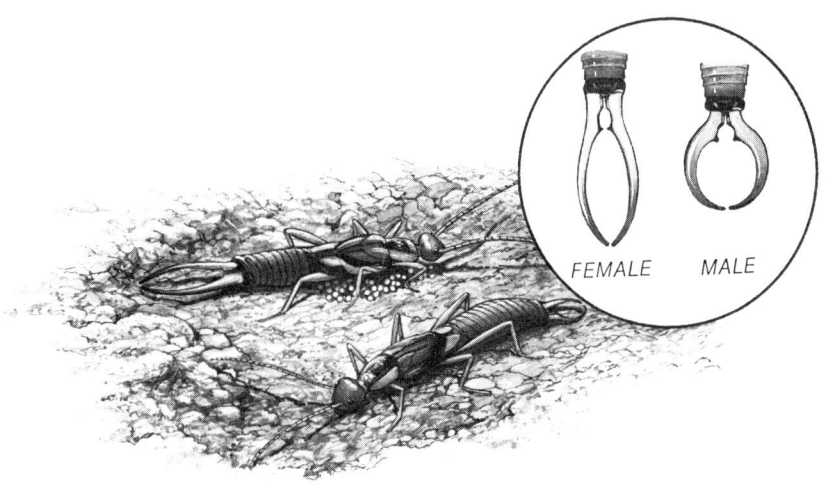

Wood Roaches

You tip a stone back and, suddenly, a flat, shiny brown insect with long antennae scuttles away—a cockroach! Why is it here, outdoors, when it could be in someone's kitchen?

The answer is that it *prefers* being outdoors. There are more than fifty species of cockroach in the United States, and only a few live indoors. In most other ways, however, all of these cockroach species are alike. They thrive in damp places. They are most active at night, and all are scavengers. Their flattened bodies enable them to squeeze into crevices and under rocks. Like sowbugs, young roaches shed their old "skins" several times as they grow bigger.

Wood roaches would probably die if you took them home and released them. In that way, at least, they are very different from the house roaches that some people dislike so much. So don't kill them (as you would a house roach). They are just another group of animals that lives successfully in hidden world ecosystems.

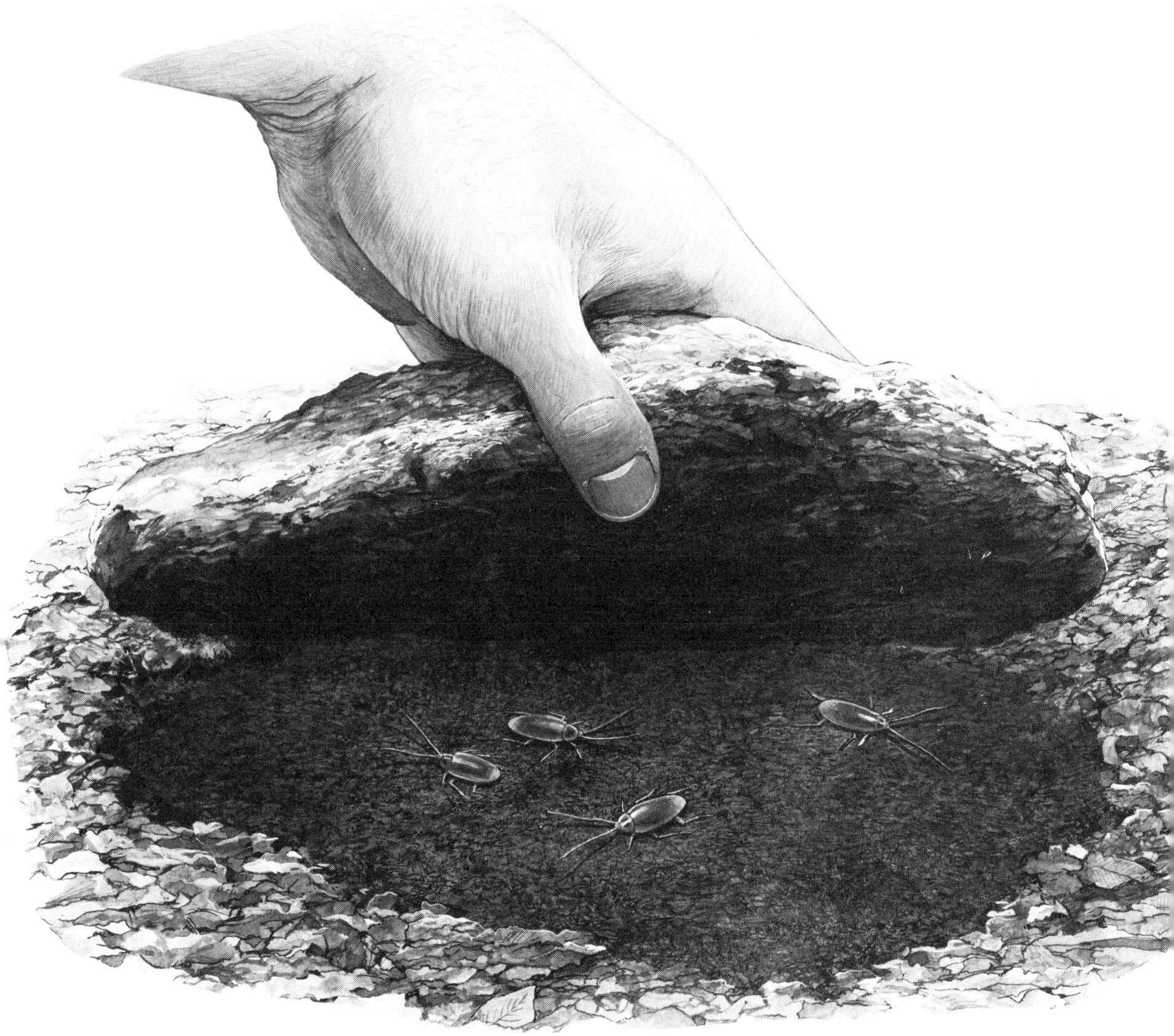

Beetles

Of all kinds of insects, beetles are the most varied and abundant. An estimated 29,000 species live in North America. Most of them spend all or part of their lives on or under the ground, so you can expect to find several kinds under rocks. You will also see their larvae (often called "grubs"). They're usually light-colored, and feed underground for a year or more before developing into pupae.

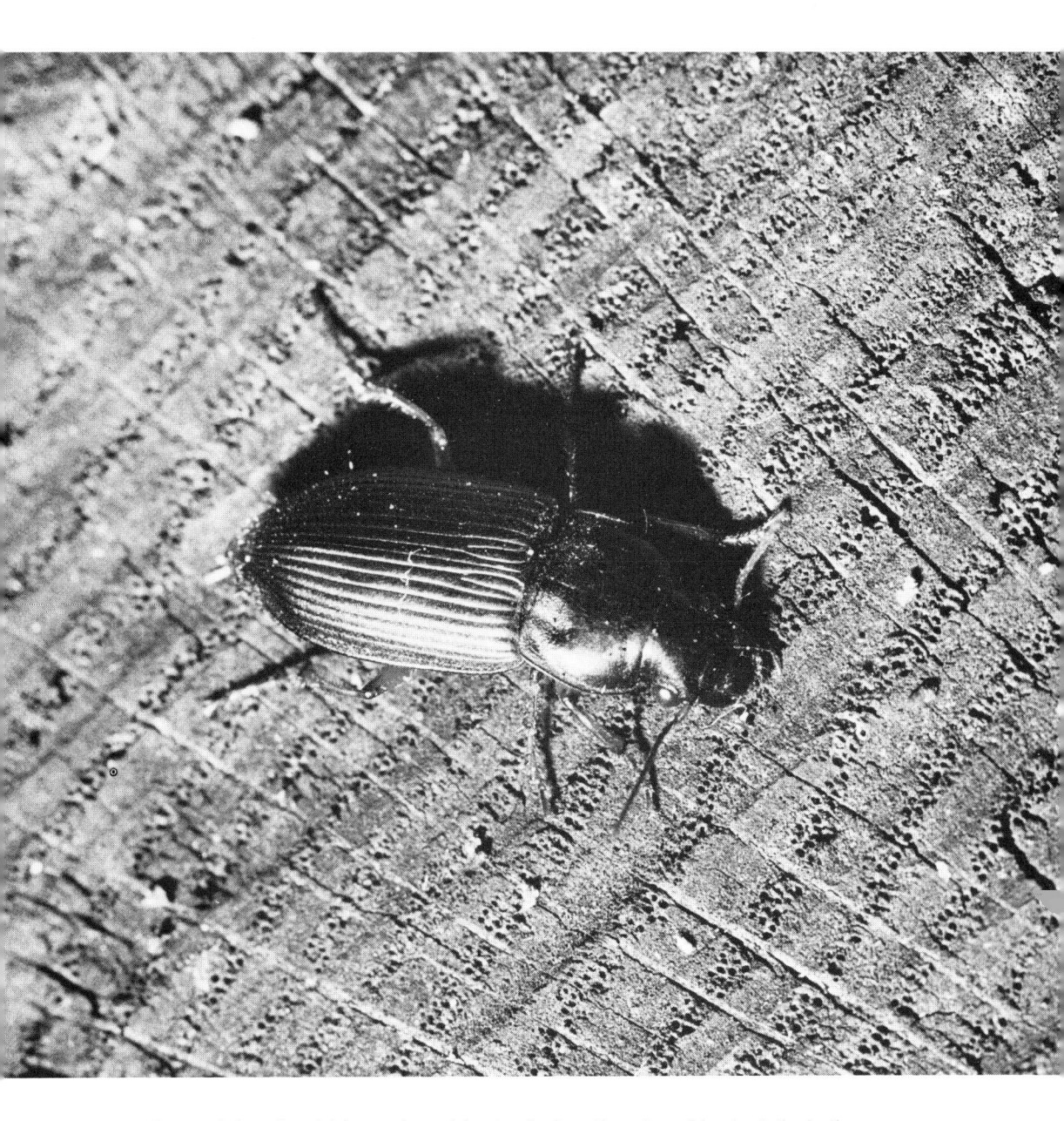

Ground beetles hide under objects during the day. Most of their lives are spent in the larval stage (left).

When you lift a rock and see a black beetle running rapidly for cover, you have probably found a ground beetle. Many kinds of ground beetles live under stones and other objects during the day. At night they roam in search of food. They are predators, with biting mouthparts, and can nip your fingers. Many of them also defend themselves with a foul odor. One group—the bombadier beetles—make a popping sound when they squirt out their liquid repellent.

The field guides listed at the end of this book will help you to identify different beetles, as well as other insects, spiders, and other animals of the hidden world. They will also help identify animals that haven't been mentioned so far. You might find a mouse nest, a toad, or a tiny red moving dot that, under a magnifying glass, becomes a mite (a relative of spiders). You may find a woolly bear caterpillar. It hides under a shelter in the autumn, eventually spins a cocoon made of its own hairs, and develops into an Isabella moth.

Female Isabella moths lay hundreds of eggs. From each egg emerges a small, "furry," red-brown caterpillar with black ends.

The caterpillar feeds and grows for several weeks.

Then it spins a cocoon made of its own hairs, stuck together with liquid silk. Watch for these cocoons under rocks and other objects.

The following spring or summer, a brown-colored Isabella moth emerges from the cocoon.

Fungi and Other Plants

Green plants cannot grow in the hidden world, since they need sunlight with which to make their food. You will, however, find the roots of grasses and other plants under rocks. You will also find fungi. Many kinds of fungi grow in moist, shady places. They include molds, yeasts, and mushrooms. Fungi come in a great variety of shapes (globs, balls, clusters—with stalks and without) and some are quite colorful. You are most likely to find these plants growing under objects where leaves or bits of wood are decaying. Most kinds of fungi get their food from once-living material. And the fungi are eaten by sowbugs, millipedes, and many other animals that live under rocks.

Under some objects, you may find white, feathery growths—the mycelium of fungi which grow on decaying leaves and wood.

WHEN YOU LOOK UNDER ROCKS IN STREAMS, ponds, and lakes, you will find very different ecosystems from those on dry land. In some ways the environment is the same—cool, dark, and damp. Very *damp*. There's too much water for sowbugs, earwigs, and centipedes. However, these conditions are ideal for other kinds of animals.

For some animals, the hidden world is a source of food. Bits of dead leaves, insects, and algae are carried along by currents and can lodge under rocks. There are also living algae and moss on the rocks or the surface under them. These foods attract scavengers and plant-eaters. They, in turn, are hunted by predators.

Rocks are shelters too. They are daytime resting places for creatures that are active at night. And they are sometimes the only calm places in areas of swift currents or crashing waves. Just as on land, the world under a rock in water is quite different from that a few inches away.

There are all sorts of other objects underwater—logs,

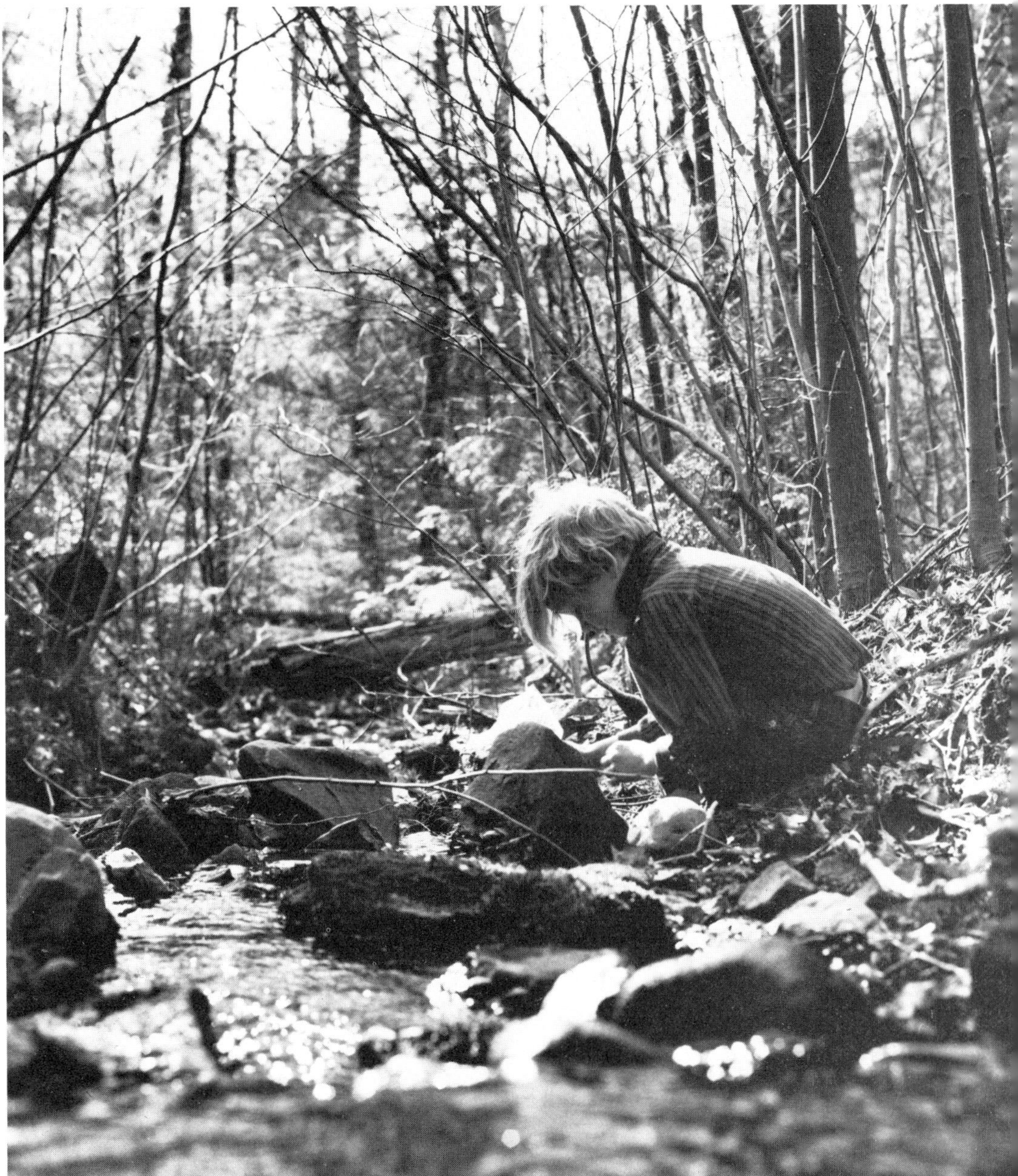

water-soaked boards, pieces of metal and trash. These objects may be ugly. Nevertheless they have value for some water animals. In 1971, a biologist studying fishes looked inside about 250 empty cans that lay underwater in streams. He found little fishes, mostly sculpins, resting in almost half of these shelters.

Some of the most common aquatic animals of the hidden world are shown on the following pages. They are all freshwater animals. Throughout North America you are likely to find them under rocks in the shallow waters of streams, ponds, and lakes, and sometimes on land close to shore. (Field guides to seashore life will help you identify animals under rocks along rocky and sandy coasts and in estuaries.)

A magnifying glass and forceps will help you explore the watery underworld. You can also catch animals with a small dip net. Boots will enable you to wade in the shallow water, but rocks and other shelters are often within easy reach of shore. On bright days, sunglasses help reduce glare from the water surface and make it easier to see the bottom.

When you lift up a rock or tip it over, be sure to look at the bottom of the rock itself. Many water animals cling there, and are hardly noticeable until they begin to move. Lifting the rock may stir up some mud or other sediment from beneath it. Wait a few minutes for the water to clear and reveal what is hidden there. Some animals may have already hidden themselves again, but you can coax them out by probing gently with a stick.

You may want to keep a notebook about your discoveries and investigations. Try to find out how the size and shape of rocks, and the tightness of their "fit" with the bottom, affects the kinds of water animals you find under them. The variety and numbers of animals reveal something about the water itself—its health. A stream or pond with a good variety of insects and other animals is free of serious pollution. It is also a delightful place to explore.

Algae and Other Plants

Algae thrive in wet places and often coat the tops and sides of rocks and other objects that lie underwater. They need sunlight in order to make food, so you won't find live algae plants underneath objects. The same is true of mosses and liverworts, which grow on rock surfaces that stick out above the water's surface. Aquatic insects creep out from the hidden world to graze on algae, mosses, and liverworts. Bits and pieces of these plants, alive and dead, are washed under rocks. You will see this material when you turn over rocks and other objects. It doesn't look like anything of much value, resembling the balls of dust that collect under beds and in closets of houses. However, this material is important food for bacteria, fungi, and some kinds of minnows and water insects.

Crayfish

Sometimes called crawfish or crabs, crayfish are close relatives of lobsters and distant relatives of the sowbugs that live under rocks on land. They are *omnivores*—eaters of just about everything, plant and animal, dead or alive. And many larger animals eat crayfish. Raccoons feel underwater for them as they prowl along the shores of streams and ponds. Crayfish are most active at night. Many species rest under stones or other objects during the day. Others dig burrows in stream banks or wet meadows.

Like other crustaceans, crayfish molt (shed) their outgrown "skins." So the "dead" crayfish you find may actually be a sort of natural litter left by a live crayfish that is hidden under a nearby rock. Its antennae, eyes, and big front claws may stick out from the hideout. Crayfish defend themselves

How to hold a crayfish

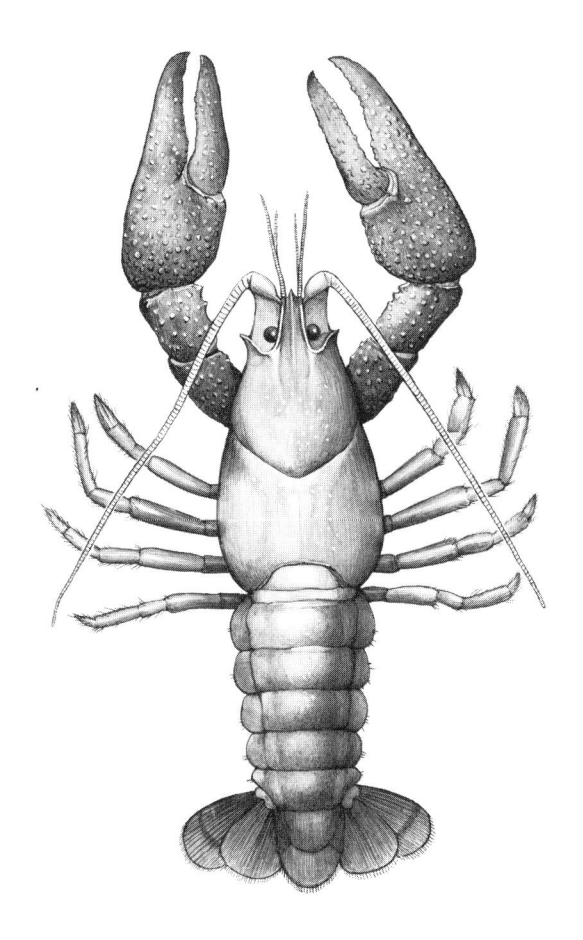

with these claws. They can also scoot rapidly backward through the water, propelled by quick flips of their tails. You can catch them with a dip net, or by grabbing their bodies just a little way behind their large claws.

Sculpins

Sculpins live in fast-flowing streams and cool, rocky ponds and lakes. They have rather squat, flattened bodies and big heads. They press close to the bottom and avoid the current as much as possible. If a sculpin flees from under a rock, you may have trouble finding it again. It is not a strong swimmer, but the color and pattern on its back blends well with its surroundings. Sculpins can even change their color. One species is able to change its mottled pattern from dark to light in three minutes or less.

Female sculpins lay masses of sticky eggs on the undersides of rocks. So do several other kinds of fish, including some darters and minnows—all the more reason to put a rock back in its original spot so the eggs are disturbed as

Sculpins are only a few inches long. This one was well hidden on a stream bottom.

little as possible. The eggs of most fish are quite small, and easily overlooked. They are noticed by many water animals, however, and are promptly eaten. Sculpins themselves eat the eggs of other fish, as well as algae and aquatic insects.

Salamanders

Salamanders are amphibians. The word *amphibian* means "double life," and some salamanders do lead double lives—part in water, part on land. There are 85 species of salamander in North America. Some live year-round on land, but they still need a damp microclimate, especially in the places where they lay their eggs.

Watch for young salamanders underwater among stones on the bottoms of streams and ponds. Only an inch or so long, they are easily overlooked. Notice the feathery growths on both sides of their necks. These are the gills with which the salamanders get oxygen from the water. Nearly all kinds of salamanders lose these gills as they develop into adults. Then they breathe with lungs, and also get oxygen through their moist skins.

The red-backed salamander (left), about three inches long, and the spotted salamander (above), up to seven inches long, both live under objects in damp places.

Leeches

Leeches are especially abundant in ponds and streams whose bottoms are covered with decaying plant material. They avoid light, often hiding under rocks and sometimes depositing cocoons of eggs there. Given the chance, certain species suck blood from humans, so people often shudder at the word *leech*. However, only a few species seek human blood. Most leeches feed on fish, frogs, turtles, or other water animals, and aren't interested in human prey.

Leeches are fascinating to watch—their rubbery bodies stretch to full length, then squeeze into a compact shape. Some species swim with a graceful up-and-down, wavelike motion. Others are poor swimmers. They "hitch" rides on larger animals, or loop along a surface as their mouth and tail suckers take turns, alternately gripping and moving. Believe it or not, leeches can be quite beautiful, with striking patterns of blues, greens, and browns.

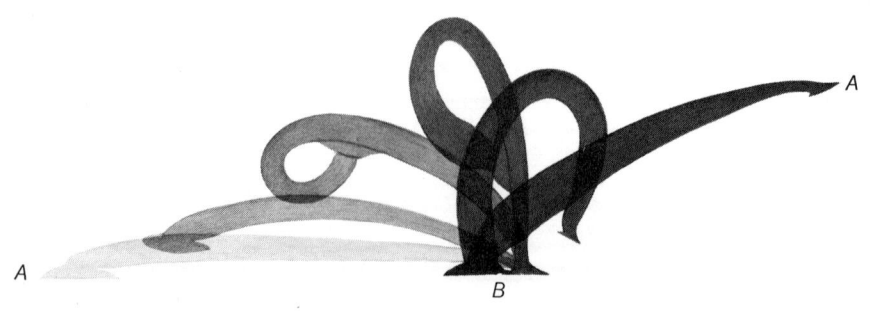

Leeches can move by letting go with one sucker (A), swinging it to a new position, then letting go with the other sucker (B).

Hellgrammites

A dip net or forceps is vital for picking up hellgrammites, for their large curved "fangs" can give your fingers a nasty nip. Hellgrammites are fierce predators of stream and pond bottoms, and often hide under stones. They sometimes reach three inches in length, and have bristling external gills sticking out from the sides of their abdomens.

A hellgrammite is an insect larva. After two or three years underwater, it forms a pupa from which later emerges a large flying adult insect—a dobsonfly. Similar but smaller larvae also hunt and hide in the hidden world. Eventually they develop into adult alderflies or fishflies.

Water Pennies

Water pennies are actually the larvae of beetles. They are usually found clinging to the underside of stones in fast-flowing water (including rocks just upriver from Niagara Falls). These larvae are well named, being round, flat, and brown—like a penny, only smaller. They eat algae and other aquatic plants.

Look for water pennies under rocks that stick partway out of the water. Rocks like these are usually chosen by female beetles when they enter the water to lay their eggs. Some kinds of riffle beetles also have clinging, pennylike larvae, though most of them are slender and long in shape.

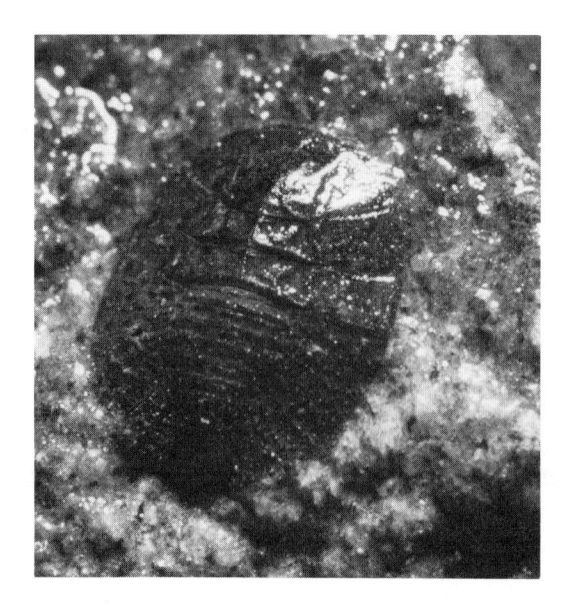

Water pennies are no more than half the size of a penny.

Caddisflies

Under some rocks you may find peculiar clusters of tiny stones or sand grains, no more than an inch long. They may seem to be part of the rock, but they are actually protective shelters, glued together with silk from mouth glands of caddisfly larvae.

Some species make shelters of sand grains or pebbles, others of bits of wood or other plant materials. The heaviest building materials are used by caddisfly larvae living in the swiftest currents; the lightweight ones in calm waters. In fact, a larva will choose heavier building materials if it is taken from its shelter and moved to a place with an increased current.

One end of a shelter is open, and the larva's head and legs emerge when it travels or eats. Most caddisfly larvae are plant-eaters or scavengers. You may see some grazing algae from the tops and sides of stones, while others find bits of food that collect under rocks.

Insect Nymphs

Large groups of common water insects develop in three stages, rather than the four (egg, larva, pupa, adult) of caddisflies, dobsonflies, and water penny beetles. The three stages are egg, nymph, and adult. Like larvae, nymphs are active, feeding, growing animals. Some are predators, some are plant-eaters, and all are an important source of food for trout and other large aquatic animals. Many kinds of nymphs are found under rocks.

Stonefly nymphs are named for their close connection with the rocks of cool streams. They have flat bodies and clawed feet that help them to hang onto rock surfaces in strong currents. Most species eat algae and bits of dead plants, though some common ones are predators. There are about 300 North American species, and one identifying character is two long "tails" that trail behind their abdomens.

A stonefly nymph

STONEFLY   MAYFLY   DAMSELFLY   DRAGONFLY

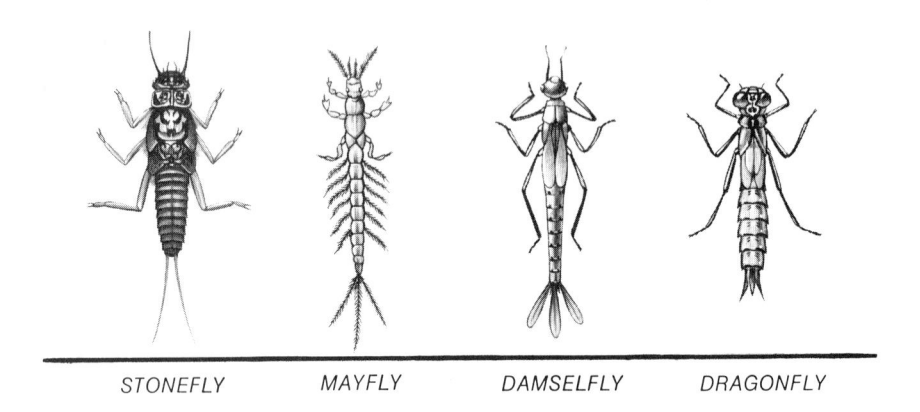

Mayfly nymphs usually have three feathery tails. There are about 500 kinds of mayflies in North America, so practically any stream or pond can harbor several species. The nymphs of dragonflies and damselflies are nearly as varied (400 North American species). Damselfly nymphs are slender and have three leaf-shaped gills at the end of their abdomens. Dragonfly nymphs are short and squat, with internal gills. They're all predators, and eat plenty of stonefly and mayfly nymphs in addition to nymphs of their own kind. Most dragonfly and damselfly nymphs live in calm or slow-flowing water. They hide among living plants or hunt along the bottom, but you will find some of them under rocks.

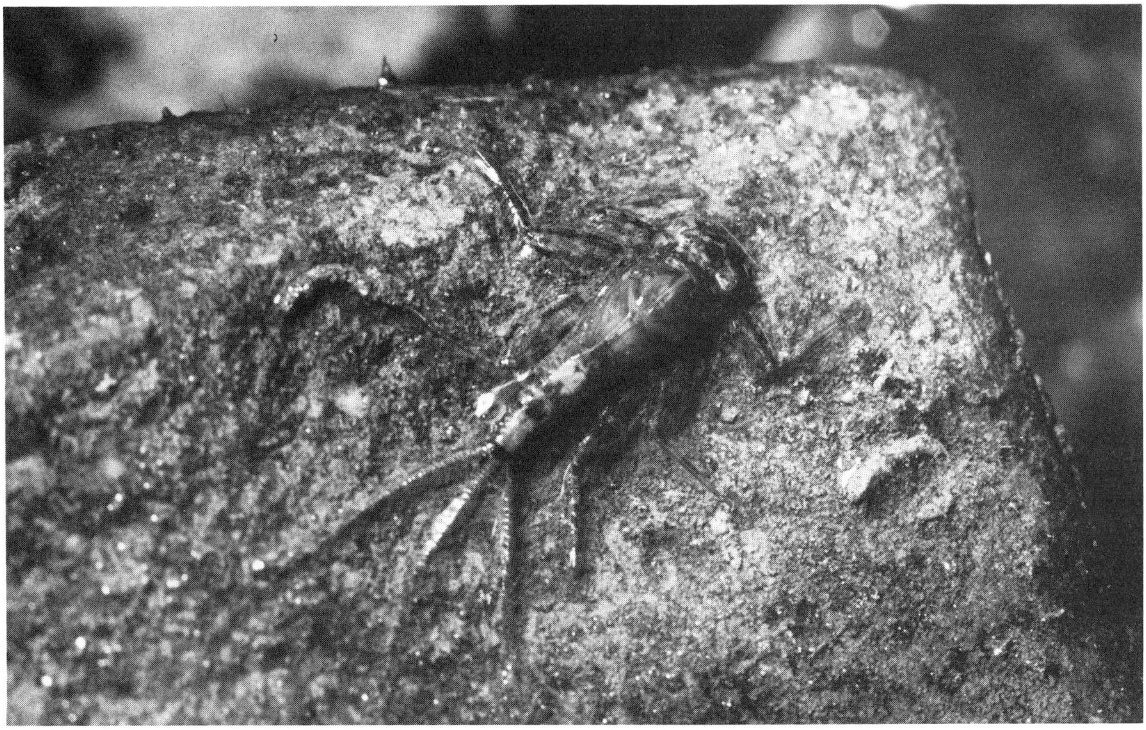

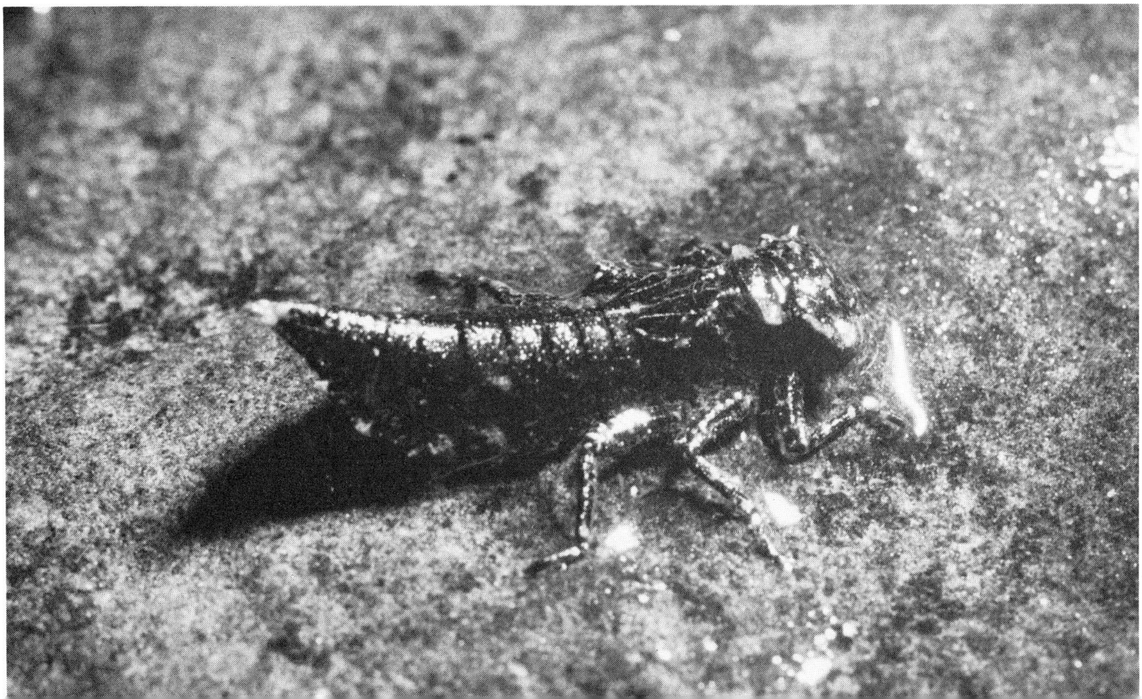

In fact, it seems that almost any small, aquatic freshwater animal can be found under a rock at some time. This includes minnows, snails, fishing spiders, and water shrews. On land or underwater, the hidden world is an extraordinary place.

Further Reading

Amos, William. *The Life of the Pond.* New York: McGraw-Hill Book Company, 1967.

Borror, Donald, and White, Richard. *A Field Guide to Insects of America North of Mexico.* Boston: Houghton Mifflin Company, 1970.

Gannon, Robert. *What's Under a Rock?* New York: E. P. Dutton & Co., Inc., 1971.

Hillcourt, William. *The New Field Book of Nature Activities and Hobbies.* New York: G. P. Putnam's Sons, 1970.

Klots, Elsie. *The New Field Book of Freshwater Life.* New York: G. P. Putnam's Sons, 1966.

Levi, Herbert, and Levi, Lorna. *A Guide to Spiders and Their Kin* (A Golden Nature Guide). New York: Golden Press, 1968.

Pringle, Laurence. *This Is a River: Exploring an Ecosystem.* New York: Macmillan Publishing Co., Inc., 1972.

Pringle, Laurence, ed. *Discovering the Outdoors: A Nature and Science Guide to Life in Fields, Forests, and Ponds.* Garden City, N.Y.: Natural History Press, 1969.

Reynolds, Christopher. *Small Creatures in My Garden.* New York: Farrar, Straus & Giroux, Inc., 1965.

Schaller, Friedrich. *Soil Animals.* Ann Arbor: The University of Michigan Press, 1968.

Schwartz, George, and Schwartz, Bernice. *Life in a Log.* Garden City, N.Y.: Natural History Press, 1972.

Usinger, Robert. *The Life of Rivers and Streams.* New York: McGraw-Hill Book Company, 1967.

Zim, Herbert, and Cottam, Clarence. *Insects: A Guide to Familiar American Insects* (A Golden Nature Guide). New York: Golden Press, 1956.

Zim, Herbert, and Reid, George. *Pond Life: A Guide to Common Plants and Animals of North American Ponds and Lakes* (A Golden Nature Guide). New York: Golden Press, 1967.

Zim, Herbert, and Smith, Hobart. *Reptiles and Amphibians: A Guide to Familiar American Species* (A Golden Nature Guide). New York: Golden Press, 1953.

Index

An asterisk (*) indicates a photograph or drawing

algae, 17, 42, 45, 49, 54, 56, 57
ants, 5, *31–*32
aphids, *30

bacteria, 45
bees, 12
beetles, 5, 11, 17, *36, *37, 38, 54, 57
black widow spiders, *28

caddisflies, *55–56
caterpillars, *39; *see also* larvae of insects
centipedes, 5, 18, *20, 42
climate, *see* microclimate
cockroaches, *see* wood roaches
cocoons, 29, 38, *39, 52
crayfish, *46–*47
crickets, 5, *31–*32

cryptosphere, 3; *see also* hidden world

damselflies, *58
dangerous animals, 12–13, 20, *28
darters, 48
dobsonflies, 53, 57
dragonflies, *58, *59

earthworms, 8, *9, 20
earwigs, 5, *14, *33, 42
ecosystems, 3, 5, 8, 10, 11, 34, 42
eggs: of ants, *29, 30; of earwigs, 33; of fishes, 48–49; of Isabella moths, *39; of leeches, 52; of salamanders, 50; of slugs, *23; of spiders, 25, *26; of water insects, 57; of water penny beetles, 54
environment, 5, 11, 42
equipment for investigating the hidden world, 11, 14, 44–45

fishes, 44, 48–49, 52
flicker, 30
forceps, *14, 44
fungi, 17, 19, *41, 45

garter snakes, *12–*13

hellgrammites, *53
hidden world: characteristics on land, 6–7, 8, 10; characteristics underwater, 42–45
humidity, 8, 10, 15, 30

insects, 20, 27, 36, 38, 42, 45, 49; see also ants, crickets, other groups
investigations of hidden world, 7–8, 10, 11, 15, 17, 44
Isabella moths, 38, *39
isopods, see sowbugs

larvae of insects, 30, *36, 53, 54, 55, 56, 57
leeches, *52
liverworts, 45
lizards, 12, 17, 31

Mars, search for life on, 10
mayflies, *58, 59
microclimate, 6–7, 8, 10, 15, 17, 23, 30, 33, 50
millipedes *18–*19, 40
minnows, 45, 48, 60
mites, 38
mosses, 42, 45

nymphs of insects, 33, *57, *58, *59, 60

omnivores, 46

pill bugs, *15
predators, 17, 19, 20, 25, 27, 38, 42, 53, 57, 58
pupae of insects, 29, 30, 36, 53, 57

raccoons, 46
roots of plants, 40

salamanders, *50–*51
scavengers, 17, 19, 21, 32, 33, 34, 42, 56
scorpions, 13
sculpins, 44, *48–*49
shrews, 7, 17, 60
slugs, 5, *21–*23
snails, 21, *22, 60
snakes, *12–*13
sowbugs, 5, 11, 15, *16, 17, 27, 34, 40, 42, 46
spiders, 17, *24, 25, *26, *28, 38, 60
springtails, *8
stoneflies, *57, *58

toads, 17, 38

water pennies, *54, 57
wolf spiders, *24, 29
wood roaches, 34, *35
woolly bear caterpillars, 38, *39

yellow jackets, 12–13

DISCARDED